> 101 letters to you

Shirly,
 I hope this book blesses you. We miss seeing you more.
   Sincerely,
   Patsy Cellier
   Jer. 29:11
   Prov. 3:5,6

101 letters to you

by:

PATSY CELLIER

TATE PUBLISHING & *Enterprises*

101 Letters to You
Copyright © 2007 by Patsy Cellier. All rights reserved.

This title is also available as a Tate Out Loud product. Visit www.tatepublishing.com for more information.

No part of this publication may be reproduced, stored in a retrieval system or transmitted in any way by any means, electronic, mechanical, photocopy, recording or otherwise without the prior permission of the author except as provided by USA copyright law.

Unless otherwise noted, Scripture quotations are taken from the *Holy Bible, King James Version,* Cambridge, 1769. Used by permission. All rights reserved.

Scripture quotations marked "TLB" are taken from *The Living Bible* / Kenneth N. Taylor: Tyndale House, © Copyright 1997, 1971 by Tyndale House Publishers, Inc. Used by permission. All rights reserved.

Scripture quotations marked "NIV" are taken from the *Holy Bible, New International Version* ®, Copyright © 1973, 1978, 1984 by International Bible Society. Used by permission of Zondervan Publishing House. All rights reserved.

Scripture quotations marked "NKJV" are taken from *The New King James Version* / Thomas Nelson Publishers, Nashville: Thomas Nelson Publishers. Copyright ©

1982. Used by permission. All rights reserved.

The opinions expressed by the author are not necessarily those of Tate Publishing, LLC.

Published by Tate Publishing & Enterprises, LLC
127 E. Trade Center Terrace | Mustang, Oklahoma 73064 USA
1.888.361.9473 | www.tatepublishing.com

Tate Publishing is committed to excellence in the publishing industry. The company reflects the philosophy established by the founders, based on Psalms 68:11, *"The Lord gave the word and great was the company of those who published it."*

Book design copyright © 2007 by Tate Publishing, LLC. All rights reserved.
Cover design by Lindsay B. Behrens
Interior design by Elizabeth A. Mason

Published in the United States of America

ISBN: 978–1–6024727–3–0
07.04.05

*This book is dedicated to my father, Syd Shaw,
who has encouraged me and believed in me all of
my life, and to my mother, Ellen Shaw, who has
read her Bible and prayed for me every day.*

Acknowledgments

I want to thank the Meadowood Baptist Church Prayer Team for their dedication to the cause of Christ, in continually lifting others up to the Lord in prayer. Without you, these letters never would have been written.

My thanks also to Iral Martin for her weekly recording of the Prayer Room Meditations onto the computer, so that we have a long term chronology of the letters. Thank you also for your patience as we corrected and finalized this book. Your help has been invaluable.

Thank you, my good friend, Ann Schley. Your prayers, encouragement, and insistence on this publication are much appreciated.

John Alexin, your expertise and patience with me as I learn to use a computer have been noteworthy. Thank you and your lovely wife, Donna.

To my family and friends go my love and thanks for cheering me on as I poured over the manuscript in making corrections.

I also want to thank Sherri Martin and Tammy Frazier for grammar consultation.

Most importantly, I want to thank and praise the Lord Jesus Christ for His Word and inspiration in the subject matter for these letters. May You receive all the glory!

Foreword

Patsy Cellier is a woman of personal prayer. She also directs the Prayer Ministry at her church. We first met while teaching Vacation Bible School many years ago. As we prayed for the students in our class, a friendship began that has grown stronger through the years. Our friendship allows us to call each other day or night with a prayer need.

We believe God's Word. In Philippians 4:6,7 we read,

> Do not be anxious about anything, but in everything, by prayer and petition, with thanksgiving, present your requests to God. And the peace of God, which transcends all understanding, will guard your hearts and your minds in Christ Jesus. (NIV)

King Solomon wrote in Proverbs 4:20–22,

> My son, pay attention to what I say; listen closely to my words. Do not let them out of your sight, keep

them within your heart, for they are life to those who find them and health to a man's whole body. (NIV)

My dear friend, Patsy Cellier, applies God's Word directly to everyday life situations. In her book, *101 Letters to You,* she demonstrates this. She listens closely to God's words, keeping them in her sight and in her heart. His words are life to her and health to her body.

May you be blessed as you read *101 Letters to You,* and may God's Word be life and health to you as well.

~Ann Schley

Introduction

As a young child, I always wanted to be a teacher. As it happened, I not only became a teacher, but I learned to sit at the feet of *The Teacher,* Jesus Christ.

Through the years of teaching, I also learned and wrote down the life lessons of the *Creator* of life, my Heavenly Father.

In the fall of 2002, I was asked to coordinate the Prayer Ministry at my church. As a way of keeping in touch with my Prayer Team, I began writing "letters" to them each week to leave in the Prayer Room. These "letters" are the basis for this book.

In the book *101 Letters to You,* you, the reader, will find that the letters are written to you as well. They are from my heart to yours, as I share the lessons I have learned from life's experiences and God's Word.

It is my prayer that you will be drawn to the feet of Jesus, and looking into His face, recognize what He wants to say to *you.*

May the book, *101 Letters to You,* lead you in that quest.

ONE

Are you ready to run a race? You may say, "I can hardly lift one foot before the other. How can I possibly run a race?"

Well, the fact that you're alive today tells us that indeed you *are* in the race. Put your feet in the starting blocks. You're on the first team. God is counting on your willingness to run. He's put *your* name on the roster.

How will you be able to run? Only by God's grace and in His strength.

> My God shall supply all your needs according to his riches in glory.
>
> Philippians 4:19

Did that say according to His poverty? No, according to His riches.

So get ready, leaning not on your own understanding, but on His provision, because the "starting gun" is about to go off—and do you know who is going to win?

YOU ARE!

TWO

Sometimes in the morning when I seem to be getting around a little slower than usual, and the cares and needs of the day begin to crowd in and urge me to "get busy," the thought comes to me that my Heavenly Father is waiting for our time together. I stop what I'm doing, take a deep breath, go to my "quiet place," and say, "Father, I'm sorry to keep you waiting."

How patient the Father is with us. Let us never keep Him waiting.

Three

If you're like I am, some days seem to be loaded with so many problems that I want to say, "Help!" But that's exactly what my Heavenly Father wants me to say, because He's there to help me.

I love the scripture, Psalm 68:19, which says,

> Blessed be the Lord, who daily loads us with benefits, even the God of our salvation.

So now, I try to remember that scripture which turns me from looking at my problems to searching for my benefits. I'm beginning to find more and more of them. I hope you will too!

Four

God's Word says,

> Be still and know that I am God...Psalm 46:10. And again, I will hear what God the Lord will speak...
> Psalm 85:8.

When children are running around wildly, an adult might say, "Be still!" Sometimes we are "running around wildly," being stressed about everyday cares. God says to us, "Be still," that we might come into His presence and know that He is God. He is in control, and He can give us peace, even when our world is in chaos.

BE STILL—AND HEAR TODAY.

Five

I am concerned that too much of our "thought life" is spent in worry. Granted, we have plenty of things to worry about. But worry doesn't change things; prayer does. Worry, stress, hurry, and fear are not from God. We must be careful about our thoughts. They affect how we view the day, how we treat other people, and how we feel.

God's Word says the following:

> ...whatsoever things are true...honest...just...pure...lovely...of good report; if there be any virtue, and if there be any praise, think on these things...and the God of peace shall be with you.
>
> Philippians 4:8, 9

GUARD YOUR THOUGHTS, AND HAVE A PEACEFUL DAY.

SIX

One time when we were visiting in Colorado, we traveled through the Eisenhower Tunnel. We could not see a light at the end of the tunnel until we went around a curve, and yet we trusted that there would be a light when we got there.

Faith is like that. Faith says that even though we are going through "dark" times in our lives, God is there to show us the "light." Indeed, He *is* the Light.

> What is faith? It is the confident assurance that something we want is going to happen. It is the certainty that what we hope for is waiting for us even though we cannot see it up ahead.
>
> Hebrews 11:1, 2 (TLB)

WALK IN FAITH TODAY. YOUR LIGHT IS AROUND THE CORNER!

SEVEN

I love to read Psalm 139. Hear these words:

> How precious also are thy thoughts unto me, O God! how great is the sum of them! If I should count them, they are more in number than the sand; when I awake, I am still with thee. Search me, O God, and know my heart: try me, and know my thoughts: And see if there be any wicked way in me, and lead me in the way everlasting.
>
> Psalm 139:17, 18, 23, 24

God, our Father, has intimate feelings about us. He knows our every thought, and still loves us! Why should we ever hesitate to bring every need to Him? He already knows our concerns, but He wants to hear from us.

Lay your cares at the Father's feet. Then walk away knowing that He's taking care of them.

Eight

To me, Christ's salvation is like the following:

I see myself standing before the judge, handcuffs holding my hands behind me. I know as I stand there that I am guilty and worthy of punishment. But as the judge brings down the gavel to sentence me, Jesus steps in front of me and receives my punishment. I deserved it, but He took it, and I am set free.

I wonder at the great love that Christ has for us. We owe Him everything. May we ever be grateful. If God never did another thing for us other than what has been done in Christ Jesus, could we ever call Him unfair?

WALK WORTHY OF YOUR SALVATION TODAY!

Nine

Did you ever think that maybe you are who you are *because* of the problems you've had in your life, not *in spite of* them?

I wonder how many times when we, in the midst of trials and tribulations, cry to the Lord, "Why?" He would say, "Because I love you!"

John 16:33b says

>...in the world you shall have tribulation: but be of good cheer; I have overcome the world.

MAY WE SEE OUR TRIALS AS AN OPPORTUNITY
TO DRAW CLOSER TO HIM.

TEN

Has it ever occurred to you that we probably wouldn't be celebrating Christmas if it were not for the events that happened at Easter?

If Jesus had not died and risen, the Christmas story would have been interesting and unusual. Jesus might have been remembered as a prophet or a godly man, but the significance of Christmas is a direct result of Easter.

Praise God for all the wonder of Christmas, as God came to earth in the form of a man. Thank God for Easter, when man was brought back to God!

George Beverly Shea sings, "O the wonder of it all! The wonder of it all! Just to think that God loves me!"

Eleven

*...unto us a child is born...*Isaiah 9:6a The scripture could have read, "unto *you* or unto *me* a child is born," because that's what happened. Just as if there had been no one else, Jesus came for us personally. Just as if *your* name were in the words, *unto (your name) a child is born.* Jesus loves us that much. He came for us individually.

So when you think of the child in the manger at Christmas time, say to yourself, "That's *my* baby; that's *my* Savior," because He is!

Twelve

In your mind picture the following scene: Jesus is walking down a narrow, dusty road on His way to Jerusalem. The throng of people is crowding all around. He stops and slowly turns part way around, and sees you far off. He looks directly at you, raises His hand to wave, and calls you by name. Then He turns back and continues down the road.

That's your personal friend. He calls to you every day. Be sure you call back—prayer is like that.

Thirteen

As I hear about the 105 million mile trip that "Spirit," our space traveler to Mars, has made, I am awed by the vastness of the universe God has created. When I consider the things scientists know about space and the many things they *don't* know, my mind expands so much I think it's going to pop! And then I think of one small insignificant person, myself, living on one of the infinitesimal places in the world. I stand in awe and silence to think that the God who made all of this—knows me. And not only does He know me, but He came down here to *die* for me. What love the Father has for us! May we think about these things and bow the knee!

> When I consider the heavens, the work of thy fingers, the moon and the stars, which thou hast ordained; what is man that thou art mindful of him? And the son of man, that thou visitest him?...O Lord our Lord, how excellent is thy name in all the earth!
>
> Psalm 8:3, 4, 9

FOURTEEN

Today I want to pull a thought from the scripture, *Thy word is a lamp unto my feet, and a light unto my path.* Psalm 119:105 I want to look at a light on a path for our meditation.

I picture a dark night. I'm traveling alone on a mountain path near a cliff. All I have is a lantern in my hand. How much of the path can I see at a time? Not very much.

Sometimes life is like that. God only shows us a little of what lies ahead for us. We are to trust Him for each step; however, we are *not* walking alone. Jesus is walking with us and *He* is holding the light. And not only that, He is walking on the "dangerous" side of the path!

May we have confidence, therefore, knowing who is leading us *and* walking beside us!

Fifteen

As I was reading the account of the Easter morning visit of the women to the tomb, something got my attention that I had not thought of before. Here is the scripture in Mark 16:5. *And entering into the sepulcher, they saw a young man sitting on the right side, clothed in a long white garment; and they were afraid.*

The angel of God was *waiting* for the women! He had rolled the stone away. Jesus was risen. He was not there. The angel was waiting to tell the women, knowing that they would come!

God is so patient with us. So many times He is waiting for us. He has done what He planned to do. He sent Jesus to die on the cross for our sins. Then He raised Him from the dead to show that He accomplished what He set out to do, and now He waits for us to come. He waits for us to come to Him in prayer. He waits for us to read His Word. He waits for us to trust that He knows best. God is so patient in waiting for us. We owe Him so much. Let's not keep Him waiting any longer.

What is God waiting for you to do? Don't keep Him waiting any longer. Do it! And may *we* have as much patience with others as God has with us!

Sixteen

As we go through the week with all the busyness it has for us, may we not only look *to* Jesus for the answers to life's stresses, but may we look *at* Him. When we look *at* Jesus, we see him looking back at us. Jesus never has His face turned *away* from us; it is always turned *toward* us. Until we realize this, we miss some of the oneness and fellowship that He seeks from us.

May this week bring you closer to Him. Walk close enough for your shoulder to touch His.

There's an old song that says, "I'll walk with God from this day on. His helping hand I'll lean upon. This is my prayer, my humble plea, may the Lord be ever with me!"

May the Lord be ever with you!

...lo, I am with you always, even unto the end of the world.

Matthew 28:20b

THIS IS HIS PROMISE, AND GOD ALWAYS KEEPS HIS WORD!

Seventeen

God looks down upon me with watchful eyes. He goes *before* me to guide me and light my path. He walks *beside* me to comfort me along the way. He follows *behind* me to keep me safe. He *surrounds* me with His love. I need nothing.

> My God shall supply all your need according to his riches in glory by Christ Jesus.
>
> Philippians 4:19.

WALK IN THE ASSURANCE OF HIS PRESENCE TODAY.

Eighteen

> I know the plans I have for you, says the Lord. They are plans for good and not for evil, to give you a future and a hope.
>
> Jeremiah 29:11

I love this scripture. I held it close to my heart when I learned that I had endometrial cancer years ago and was preparing for surgery. It encouraged me to know that God had future plans for me and that I was healed. And indeed, I am.

Today, however, I realized that God has a plan for me *each* day.

I get up in the morning thinking that I'm going to do "this or that" today, only to find that His plans include something else. I might need to write a note or call someone, or a person may cross my path who needs to talk to me. The plans that *I* had for the day may not get accomplished, but what a joyous day it is to be guided by Him and to know at the end of the day that He is satisfied.

Be attentive to what God's plan is for you each day. It will be much more fulfilling than your own!

NINETEEN

> ...forgetting those things which are behind, and reaching forth unto those things which are before, I press toward the mark for the prize of the high calling of God in Christ Jesus.
>
> Philippians 3:13, 14

We are to leave our past sins, our old ways of doing things, our hang-ups, our griefs, our anger, our unforgiveness (of ourselves and others), our pain, our disappointments, our hatreds, and all other "garbage" at Jesus' feet. We are to walk away! Those things are passed! We are not to go there again!

Now, we are to reach forth to those things God has *before* (ahead of) us!

My friends, go forth with diligent expectations of the great things that God has "ahead" for you. You will not be disappointed!

Twenty

Think of the problem that is most pressing on your mind today. Do you feel that you have tried everything that you can think of to solve the problem but nothing seems to work?

When that happens, remember the following scripture:

> For my thoughts are not your thoughts, neither are your ways my ways, saith the Lord. For as the heavens are higher than the earth, so are my ways higher than your ways, and my thoughts than your thoughts.
>
> Isaiah 55:8, 9

We may have exhausted all of *our* ways to solve a problem. Now we need to wait for God's way. It *will* be revealed—in His time. If we had asked Him *first,* the answer would have come sooner!

Twenty One

If we do not read God's Word, then we don't know what God would have us do in a certain circumstance. When we read His Word, we know what God's opinion is and what we should do.

> Your word I have hidden in my heart, that I might not sin against you...I have inclined my heart to perform your statutes forever, to the very end.
>
> Psalm 119:11, 112 (NKJV)

Once we recognize God's will, then we must be obedient—to the end (every time).

> WALK IN HIS WORD, AND YOU WILL
> FULFILL HIS PURPOSES FOR YOU.

Twenty Two

When I come home from a vacation, or in my case, come home from a grandchild's birthday in Colorado, I think about what lies ahead, getting back to my routine.

Recently, I contemplated my future and thought back to my birth. As my mother was in labor, the doctor told my dad that they had lost the baby's heartbeat, and they were afraid that the baby would be stillborn. My dad says he's still thrilled as he thinks back to the loud cry he heard as I was born. God had spared my life. He had a plan for me.

This time as I returned home from Colorado, I thought, "Lord, help me to *be* all that You planned for me to be, and *do* all that You planned for me to do."

> You made all the delicate, inner parts of my body, and knit them together in my mother's womb…You were there while I was being formed in utter seclusion!

You saw me before I was born and scheduled each day of my life before I began to breathe...Search me, O God, and know my heart; test my thoughts. Point out anything you find in me that makes you sad, and lead me along the path of everlasting life.

Psalm 139:13–16, 23, 24 (TLB)

Think back to a time when God's intervention was apparent in your life. I hope your prayer is the same as mine.

TWENTY THREE

Have you had a time lately, or maybe in the past, where you went out of your way to do something nice for someone, and they didn't even notice or didn't care or didn't thank you?

When that happens, and it will, remind yourself of the following scriptures—and smile!

> When a servant comes in from plowing or taking care of the sheep, he doesn't just sit down and eat, but first prepares his master's meal and serves him his supper before he eats his own. And he is not even thanked, for he is merely doing what he is supposed to do.
>
> Luke 17:7–9 (TLB)

> And I, the king, will tell them, 'When you did it to these my brothers, you were doing it to me!
>
> Matthew 25:40 (TLB).

JESUS ALWAYS NOTICES—AND IS PLEASED!

Twenty Four

● ● ● ● ● ● ● ● ● ●

One morning I woke up, but before I could get out of bed, stresses, worries, the unknown, came flooding over me. It was a cloudy day. I could tell even before I opened the blinds. Then I realized that the sun *was* shining. The sun *always* shines, but we don't always see it! The clouds may be in the way.

I thought about God always being there. Sometimes it doesn't "appear" that He is, but He is! So we must not let the "clouds" of our day cause us to doubt the "Son's" presence.

> I am the light of the world: he that followeth me shall not walk in darkness, but shall have the light of life.
> John 8:12

Twenty Five

I believe in miracles. Jesus paying for our sins is a miracle of God's love and grace toward each of us who has accepted Him as Savior and Lord.

I want to tell you about a special situation that happened when the Singing ChurchWomen were in Budapest, Hungary.

We were getting ready to begin the service in Heroes' Square where 25,000 people had gathered for a Jesus Rally. We were first on the program. As we were on stage waiting to sing, it was very hot. The sun was directly on my face. It felt like I was getting an instant sunburn. As I was standing there, I looked up at the sky. It was a beautiful blue with no clouds in sight. In my mind I prayed, "Lord, please send a cloud to cover the sun while we sing. It is so hot and we can hardly see." Ten or fifteen minutes passed, and Bill Green, our director, stood to lead our singing. At that moment a slight gentle breeze blew momentarily across my face. I looked up to see that a small cloud had moved in covering the sun. It was not a big puffy cloud but a small one just the right size. The cloud remained there until we completed our songs; then it moved away. The next day I looked at my face for sunburn. No sunburn. Jesus calmed the storm one time when He was in a boat, and God brought a cloud when I was in a foreign land. What an awesome God we serve. How great is the Father's love for us!

TWENTY SIX

Last Friday was my birthday. At 11:15 p.m. as I was about to fall asleep, I thought about all the years I have lived, and I thanked God for them. In my mind I took God's hand and thanked Him for the year that lies before me. I thanked Him for all the blessings and special times that would come. I thanked Him that in times of trouble or need, He would be there.

What a great God we serve and oh how He loves His children—aren't you glad you're one too!

Song:
"Oh how He loves you and me,
Oh how He loves you and me,
He gave His life, what more could He give?
Oh how He loves you and me."

For God so loved the world, that he gave his only begotten son; that whosoever believeth in him, should not perish, but have everlasting life.

John 3:16

Twenty Seven

> Let the words of my mouth and the meditation of my heart be acceptable in thy sight, O Lord, my strength, and my redeemer.
>
> Psalm 19:14

We usually think of "meditation" as having to do with thinking about things of God—meditating on the scripture—meditating on something godly. But meditation could be "whatever we let our mind dwell on." If that's the case, then we need to think about "what our mind is thinking about."

If we are letting our "mind" say bad things about someone who just got our parking place, or our promotion, or "their way" in our home, then we need to STOP those thoughts and bring them back to meditations that would be pleasing to God.

How do we do that? It is a continuous process that begins with recognizing what our mind is doing.

When we recognize that we are thinking "ungodly" thoughts, we say, "I'm sorry, God. Help me to make the meditations of my heart be what is pleasing in Your sight."

We will find that the words of our mouth will automatically become more pleasing to God when the meditations of our heart are God-ward. May our minds be filled with godly meditations today!

Twenty Eight

In May of 1999 there was a severe tornado in the area where we lived. In fact, our neighbors had to rebuild their home because of the damage. On the corner of their property near the street was a very tall, thin tree. The tornado left the tree broken, jagged, without leaves, and seemingly without life. For the last few years, we have looked at that tree thinking that someone should cut it down. It looked so bad.

This week as I took a neighborhood walk, I suddenly stopped and looked up at the tree as I walked by it. It was lovely—full of branches and leaves, tall, as if reaching to the sky, thanking God for its life!

"Wow! What a lesson," I thought. "We are like that tree. Our lives are battered, broken, without hope of life or productivity. Then Jesus comes along and gives us new life."

I'm glad God didn't let someone "cut me down" when I was lost and without hope. He gave me His new life, and now I live in Him!

> He has made all things beautiful in his time...
> Ecclesiastes 3:11a

> Therefore if any man be in Christ, he is a new creature. Old things are passed away; behold all things are become new.
> II Corinthians 5:17

WALK IN YOUR NEW LIFE TODAY FORGETTING THE THINGS THAT LAY BEHIND.

TWENTY NINE

In my family birthdays are a big deal! My mother just had a birthday. I invited all of the family to come to dinner at my house. All of my married life I have cooked for my family. It is not my comfort zone. I'm usually not very confident about everything turning out just right, but I do it anyway because it is important to my family.

When the meal had ended and the homemade chocolate pie had been consumed, my dad knowingly looked at me and said, "Who made all of this food?" I smiled and said, "I did." He replied, "Gooood food!" I guess that's why I do it—to hear, "Well done."

I pondered the moment and reflected on the scripture, *Well done, thou good and faithful servant...*Matthew 25:21a

If it blesses me to have my dad give approval for something I've done, how much more it will bless me to have my Savior one day say what the master of the servant said,

Well done, thou good and faithful servant: thou hast been faithful over a few things, I will make thee ruler over many things: enter into the joy of thy lord.

Matthew 25:21

MAY WE SPEND *EACH* DAY LOOKING FOR A "WELL DONE!" FROM THE LORD.

Thirty

> I will instruct thee and teach thee in the way which thou shalt go: I will guide thee with mine eye.
>
> Psalm 32:8

As a teacher in a classroom, I could direct students behavior many times "with my eye" without saying a word. I could look with approval, adding a smile. I could look discerningly as if to say, "I saw that!" I could simply look at a student who was misbehaving, and he would stop.

God says He will guide us with His eye.

For a student to get the message I was sending with my eye, the student would have to be *looking* at me.

If we are to receive God's guidance, we have to be *looking* at Him! How do we do that? We look at Him through His Word to guide us. We look at Him in prayer.

We can never look at God when He's not looking back at us! Look to God this week and receive your instructions.

> Be ye not as the horse or as the mule, which have no understanding...
>
> Psalm 32:9a (No comment needed.)

Thirty One

Have you ever thought about the availability of God? Have you ever contemplated His being everywhere at the same time—His omnipresence?

Our daughter called one morning early to say that our grandson was in pain. She described the symptoms, but we were of no help in the diagnosis. She asked for prayer and discernment.

As Clayton and I prayed, I realized several things. We have to wait for the doctor to call us back, but we can go directly to the Healer! We don't have to wake God up or wait for Him to get back to us. He's always there! Not only is He with *us,* but He's with *them,* the people for whom we're praying. God heard our prayer. Yes! But He didn't have to leave us to go to our grandson. He was already *there* as well! Soon, Sue Ann called back and said that Jason was feeling better and was asking for "pancakes."

Song:
"O the wonder of it all; the wonder of it all,
Just to think that God loves me.
The wonder of it all, the wonder of it all,
Just to think that God loves me!"

GOD TRULY DOES LOVE US, AND HE'S *WHEREVER* HIS CHILDREN ARE.

THIRTY TWO

This summer my grandson, Johnathan, went to church camp for the first time. As I was driving him to the church, I told him that I would be praying for him while he was gone. I would pray for him when he got up in the morning and when he went to bed at night. Then I paused and said, "...and probably in between." I think about my children and grandchildren often. They are very precious to me.

I pondered that thought and remembered the scripture that said,

> How precious are thy thoughts unto me, O God! How great is the sum of them. If I should count them, they are more in number than the sand...
>
> Psalm 139:17, 18

Our God is not off somewhere out of our reach. He's very near. He's thinking about us even now. We know He is because we can talk to Him at any time.

What would our lives be like if we thought about Him as often as He thinks about us? Changed!

Thiry Three

Today I was reading some things I wrote many years ago. They still speak to my heart. I hope they speak to you as well.

Only those who can cry can know the value of a smile.

God didn't promise to give us all that we ask for, but He promised not to withhold any good thing from them that walk uprightly.

How do you *know* if you're going in the right direction? You *know* if you're following Jesus.

Peace is standing in the presence of God; seeing Him smile, we know everything is all right.

Thirty Four

Clayton and I were meeting some friends for dinner one night. Clayton turned on I-40 and I thought the eating place was off of I-240. I questioned the turn, but he said, "This is the right place." Clayton is usually very good at directions, so I remained silent. All the time I was thinking, "This is the wrong way." Even though I thought he had made a mistake, because of past experience, I trusted him. I thought, "If he's wrong, he'll figure it out. He doesn't need me to say anything else."

We arrived at the eating place on time. Clayton had known exactly what he was doing. He didn't need my help.

Aren't we like this with God many times? We want to question what He's doing, or give Him advice, only to find that He knew exactly what He was doing and never needed our advice.

I hope the next time that happens to us, we will remember our past experience with God, relax, and let Him work! He'll get us where we're supposed to be, and we'll always be on time!

> Trust in the Lord with all thine heart; and lean not unto thine own understanding. In all thy ways, acknowledge him and he shall direct thy paths.
>
> Proverbs 3:5, 6

THIRTY FIVE

Recently we have been looking into Long Term Care policies. Thinking about who will take care of us when we are "old" is a very scary thing. We don't know what the future holds, so it's hard to plan for it. I don't want anyone to have to take care of me, and it's frightening to wonder if anyone will. In the midst of these worries, I am stopped short as I remember the following song:

> "God will take care of you,
> Through every day,
> O'er all the way;
> He will take care of you.
> God will take care of you."

If God takes care of us throughout our lives, why would He *not* take care of us when we are about to depart this world to be with Him in eternity?

> The Lord will keep you from all harm—he will watch over your life; the Lord will watch over your coming and your going both now and forevermore.
>
> Psalm 121:7, 8 (NIV)

Thirty Six

When I'm getting ready to go somewhere, I sometimes find that I have either waited too long to start getting ready or didn't allow enough time. Clayton is very patient with me. He never gets upset or says anything to me to hurry me along, but he will come into the room and pretend to be doing something else. I get the message.

Is God waiting for you to do something that He's told you to do? Have you been putting it off? Has He stepped into your presence time and time again to remind you of what He has said? Think about it. God is so patient with us, but we often keep Him waiting. Don't keep Him waiting any longer. Be about your Father's work!

Jesus said,

> ...I must be about my Father's business.
> Luke 2:49b

WE ARE GOD'S CHILDREN TOO!

Thirty Seven

Hear what Solomon says about our words:

> The mouth of a righteous man is a well of life...
>
> Proverbs 10:11a

> In the multitude of words there wanteth not sin: but he that refraineth his lips is wise.
>
> Proverbs 10:19

> A soft answer turneth away wrath: but grievous words stir up anger.
>
> Proverbs 15:1

> ...a word spoken in due season, how good is it!
>
> Proverbs 15:23b

> Even a fool, when he holdeth his peace, is counted wise; and he that shutteth his lips is esteemed a man of understanding.
>
> Proverbs 17:28

A word fitly spoken is like apples of gold in pictures of silver.

Proverbs 25:11

A fool uttereth all his mind: but a wise man keepeth it in till afterwards.

Proverbs 29:11

May we choose our words wisely this week so that we may be a blessing to those around us. May our words bring peace and not strivings. May they bring joy and comfort to those who are hurting. May they bring songs of thanksgiving to bless our Father's heart.

Thirty Eight

As a cold front approached our area last week, it became evident that I needed to repot some patio plants and bring them indoors immediately.

I bought a new, larger pot for a beautiful fern that had grown through the summer. I prepared the pot with lots of nourishing potting soil. I ran a kitchen knife around the inside of the old pot to release the plant and began pulling it out of the pot. It wouldn't budge. I pulled and tugged to no avail. The plant wanted to hold on to its old pot! It didn't realize that I had prepared wonderful things for it to help it grow even more next year. It was content with things as they were. (You see where I'm going with this.)

As I pondered this situation, I wondered how many "pots" *we* are holding on to, content with things as they are: pots of pride, unforgiveness, and self-centeredness, when God has new, fresh, better pots waiting for us, if only we'll let go.

Do you realize that God has "better" plans for you than you do for yourself? Take a moment to ask Him what they are, and tell Him you'll let go of your "old pots" to let Him work.

> ...let us lay aside every weight, and the sin which doth so easily beset us, and let us run with patience the race that is set before us, looking unto Jesus the author and finisher of our faith...
>
> Hebrews 12:1, 2

Watch out for any "pot holes" Satan may send your way this week!

P.S. Clayton helped me get the fern out of its pot. It's happy in its new pot in a sunny place inside the house!

Thirty Nine

Peace—peace—peace—but there is no peace, or is there?

We pray for peace in the world.
We pray for peace in Iraq.
We pray for peace in our families.
We pray for peace in our own hearts.
In the world we find no peace.
In Iraq there is no peace.
In our families, we have peace for a season.
But in our hearts we *can* have peace.
Hear the Word of the Lord:

Thou wilt keep him in perfect peace whose mind is stayed on thee...

Isaiah 26:3

Peace I leave with you; my peace I give unto you; not as the world giveth, give I unto you...

John 14:27

These things I have spoken unto you that in me, ye might have peace...

John 16:33

Peace is God's promise, and it is a Gift of the Spirit. We can't always control our circumstances or change decisions that others make, but we can have peace in the *midst* of our circumstances. It is God's promise to us if we look *to* Him and *at* Him and receive *from* Him.

MAY YOU LIVE IN PEACE TODAY.

Forty

When traveling on I-240, I always enjoy looking at the trees. It bothers me when large numbers of trees are cut down in a housing area. I love growing things. They are part of God's creation.

As I traveled along, I began looking at the trees individually instead of a "forest of trees." I never had noticed how different each tree is from another, even one of the same species. They are different in size, shape, even color during the fall season.

I realized that God doesn't look at us as "humanity" or "people of the earth." He doesn't see us as "people of the United States" or "of Oklahoma" or "in the Cellier family." God sees us as individuals; people He made one by one. We are special to Him. He calls us by our own name. He calls us His children.

If that is so, why do we worry so much?

> ...behold the fouls of the air...your Heavenly Father feeds them. Consider the lilies of the field...even Solomon was not arrayed like one of these.
>
> Matthew 6:26, 28

What are we to do?

> Seek first the kingdom of God and his righteousness: and all these things shall be added unto you.
>
> Matthew 6:33

> So don't be anxious about tomorrow, God will take care of your tomorrow too. Live one day at a time.
>
> Matthew 6:34 (TLB)

FORTY ONE

When you cry to God—when you wonder if He is there—when you think your problems are overwhelming, hear what His Word says:

> Fear not, for I have redeemed thee. I have called thee by thy name. Thou art mine. When thou passeth through the waters, I will be with thee; and through the rivers, they shall not overflow thee. When thou walkest through the fire, thou shalt not be burned; neither shall the flame kindle upon thee.
>
> Isaiah 43:1b, 2

He has redeemed us, called us by our very own name, and said that we are His—what more could we ask?

Forty Two

Have you ever thought about the strength of an eagle? It can soar far above the earth, spot an animal on the ground or a fish in the ocean, swoop down, and pick it up. It can then propel its own body weight, plus that of its prey right back into the sky. Wow!

God says we can be like that.

> But they that wait upon the Lord shall renew their strength; they shall mount up with wings as eagles; they shall run, and not be weary; and they shall walk and not faint.
>
> Isaiah 40:31

So when you're feeling weak emotionally, spiritually, or physically, remember God's promise to you. Turn to Him, and He will lift you up with His strength which is even mightier than the eagle's!

Forty Three

I seem to be prone to getting colds. It's as if the germs see me in a crowd and say, "Hey, Patsy's here. Let's get her!"

When a cold attacks me, I've found that if I listen to my body, I get well sooner. God has given us a good immune system if we will let it do its job. Therefore, when I begin to have symptoms, I go to bed and rest, take my Coldeze, drink extra water, and pray for God's healing. I usually am better in a few days instead of weeks.

Sin is like those cold germs. It enters our life, and we are content to leave it alone. It, taking the opportunity, gets worse.

When we first notice our sin, we must repent of it. We must let God's healing grace redeem us; then we are renewed. We feel better. Our sin is gone, and we get back to the work He called us to do.

Don't live in a "germy" sin environment. Be continually renewed through prayer each day.

> Be not conformed to this world: but be transformed by the renewing of your mind, that you may prove what is that good and acceptable and perfect will of God.
>
> Romans 12:2

Forty Four

When we come before the Lord to pray, we need to be like Isaiah as he saw himself and said,

> ...woe is me! For I am undone; because I am a man of unclean lips: for mine eyes have seen the King, the Lord of Hosts.
>
> Isaiah 6:5

When Isaiah saw himself compared to who God was, he said, *Woe is me, I am a sinner.* Having seen himself thus, he knew something needed to be done.

> Then flew one of the seraphims...with tongs from the altar...and laid it upon my mouth and said,...thine iniquity is taken away, and thy sin purged.
>
> Isaiah 6:6, 7

When Isaiah's sin was forgiven, he could answer God's question, *Whom shall I send, and who will go for us?* Isaiah could reply, *Here am I, send me.* Isaiah 6:8

We are not worthy to pray for others until we repentantly acknowledge our own sin and are forgiven; then we can approach the throne of God with a clean heart.

MAY OUR LIPS BE PURGED WITH FIRE THIS WEEK, SO THAT WE MAY BOTH PRAY AND SPEAK GOD'S NAME.

Forty Five

> For we have not an high priest which cannot be touched with the feeling of our infirmities; but was in all points tempted like as we are, yet without sin. Let us therefore come boldly unto the throne of grace, that we may obtain mercy, and find grace to help in time of need.
>
> Hebrews 4:15, 16

When Queen Esther went into the presence of King Xerxes in his throne room, she hoped he would stretch out his scepter toward her. By stretching out his scepter, king Xerxes would be showing that he accepted the queen and would hear her petition.

When we pray, we enter God's throne room. As we come into His presence, not only is His scepter outstretched toward us, but He rises from His throne and comes to greet us with open arms!

FORTY SIX

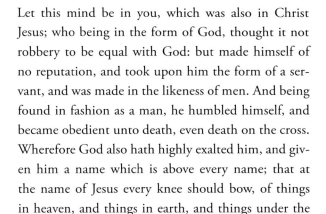

Let this mind be in you, which was also in Christ Jesus; who being in the form of God, thought it not robbery to be equal with God: but made himself of no reputation, and took upon him the form of a servant, and was made in the likeness of men. And being found in fashion as a man, he humbled himself, and became obedient unto death, even death on the cross. Wherefore God also hath highly exalted him, and given him a name which is above every name; that at the name of Jesus every knee should bow, of things in heaven, and things in earth, and things under the earth; and that every tongue should confess that Jesus Christ is Lord, to the glory of God the Father.

Philippians 2:5–11

This is the Christ of Christmas!

Forty Seven

As I went through my daddy's belongings after his passing, I was reminded that daddy really had no earthly "treasures." He had files on his children and grandchildren showing his pride in our accomplishments. He treasured cards and letters that we had sent him, but he had nothing of material value in which he took pride.

I'm not a person who collects many things, so I understand my daddy's thinking. As I was reading the Psalms for comfort in this stressful time, tears came to my eyes. I gathered up my Bible and held it close to me and said to the Lord, "Your Word is my greatest treasure."

If an enemy took everything that you had but one thing, what would you *have* to keep?

> Lay not up for yourselves treasures upon earth, where moth and rust doth corrupt and where thieves break through and steal: But lay up for yourselves treasures in heaven, where neither moth nor rust doth corrupt and where thieves do not break through nor steal: For where your treasure is, there will your heart be also.
>
> Matthew 6:19–21

Forty Eight

When I'm at the breakfast table, I can watch the birds come to the bird feeder and birdbath in the backyard. My favorite birds are the cardinals. I like to see them up close through binoculars.

One morning I made the following observation: A singing bird has no fear. If he were afraid, he would not be singing. If a predator were near, he would not sing and bring attention to himself. If he were hungry, he would not be content—a singing bird is at peace with the world.

Listen for a singing bird, for while you are quiet, you may hear the voice of God!

> Be still and know that I am God.
>
> Psalm 46:10

Forty Nine

Wait on the Lord: be of good courage, and he shall strengthen thine heart: wait, I say, on the Lord.

Psalm 27:14

Wait...be of good courage . . .

For most of us, "waiting" is probably *not* our best asset. How are we apt to behave while we are waiting? Are we apt to be in a dither, pace the floor, wring our hands, worry, fret, complain, be unhappy with the Lord for not doing something "now"?

What does the Word say? *Be of good courage.* Have a good attitude while you wait. Uh, oh—now I'm meddling, aren't I? (But I'm talking to myself as well.) What does the Word say will happen?...*and he shall strengthen your heart.* How true that is! Don't you find that when you leave something in God's hands, you are strengthened? Your steps have a spring to them. A smile appears on your face. You feel better!

Let's remind each other to *be of good courage* while we wait. He promises to strengthen us, and God doesn't lie. He keeps His Word!

Fifty

As I was preparing to visit my mom one day, I asked Clayton to find a nail for me so I could hang a small clock on the wall of mom's room.

Clayton laid out two nails of different sizes for me to use. As I looked at the thin nails needed to hang something lightweight on a wall, I thought of the size of nail that would be needed to hang something heavy—like a person—on a cross. That nail would have to be very big. It would hurt a lot if hammered into one's hands—and feet. Tears came to my eyes when I thought of how much that would hurt. It hurt Jesus a whole lot. It was not only the weight of His body that hung on the cross, but the weight of the sin of the world—my sin included. That weight hurt even more, but love hung there as well. And love was stronger!

FIFTY ONE

> The first day of the week cometh Mary Magdalene early, when it was yet dark, unto the sepulchre and seeth the stone taken away from the sepulchre.
>
> John 20:1

Put yourself in Mary's place on the third day after Jesus' crucifixion. She was in the garden crying, when suddenly Jesus appeared to her. At first she didn't recognize Him; then she realized it was her Lord—He was alive!

When it's our time to go to heaven, we'll see Jesus too. But we won't be surprised—because we know He's risen!

Fifty Two

Who do you talk to?

You talk to your family. You talk to your friends. You talk to people at work.

Do you sometimes talk to yourself?

Are those thoughts often complaints or worries or criticisms?

The other day I found myself doing that, and I said to myself, "Stop talking to yourself, and start talking to God!"

We think we don't have enough time to talk to God, but we spend a lot of time talking to ourselves. Those thoughts often cause us to be more worried and upset. There's a song that says the following:

"Have a little talk with Jesus,
Tell him all about your troubles,
You will find a little talk with Jesus makes it right."

Let's practice *stopping* our negative mind conversations, and *start* having a healthy conversation with the Lord. We'll probably be spending a *lot* of time with the Lord that way!

Fifty Three

Though the storms of life may gather and there seems to be no peace,
We know the sun will shine again and the thunder indeed will cease.

Have you ever noticed that following a terribly stormy night, a beautiful, calm, sunny morning greets you the next day? Think about this "life lesson": storms are not continual; they last for a short time, then they're gone.

Why is it that when we are in the midst of a "stormy" time in our life, we don't remember that the storm *will* end, and the sun *will* shine again? Actually the "Son" is even there in the midst of the storm.

> And he arose, and rebuked the wind, and said unto the sea, Peace, be still. And the wind ceased, and there was a great calm.
>
> Mark 4:39

LET THE "SON" CALM THE STORM IN YOU.

Fifty Four

> My voice shalt thou hear in the morning, O Lord; in the morning will I direct my prayer unto thee, and will look up.
>
> Psalm 5:3

It's morning, Lord, and I don't know what the day holds for me. But I know You go before me. You walk beside me. You watch over me. You walk behind me. Your arm is around me. Your love enfolds me. So I can step out into the day—because I have prayed.

FIFTY FIVE

A message from our Heavenly Father:

Why do you worry so?

You worry about next year—and next month—tomorrow and whether you will sleep well tonight. Come.

I am already there. I know what you will be doing next year, and next month, and tomorrow, and you will sleep tonight. Come.

You worry about your health—and your money—and your friends and family. Come.

I am your health, and your finances are many. I am your best friend, and I hold your family in My care.

I not only know the answers to your questions about the future, but I am already there. Come.

So lay aside your worries, and just come.

Fifty Six

When do you think "everlasting life" or "eternity" begins?

We usually associate these terms with the event of death. We will enter eternity. We will live eternally—but when we accept Jesus as our Savior, we begin eternal "life." Right now and from now on, we are living eternally with Him.

Think about that. There's no stopping. There's no ending of our walk with the Savior. We just step over the line at death, and we're in a new dimension of life.

What a relief! Eternity is not a place. It's longevity. We're in it now. We're in it with Jesus!

Billy Graham says the following concerning heaven: "Someday you will read or hear that Billy Graham is dead. Don't believe a word of it! I shall be more alive then than I am now. I will have just changed my address. I will have gone into the presence of God."

The Apostle Paul says,

> For me to live is Christ and to die is gain.
>
> Philippians 1:21

Fifty Seven

I like to talk to my children and grandchildren as often as I can. It helps me to know what is going on in their lives and gives me an opportunity to say, "I love you."

I told God that I wished He would speak to me often like that. He said that He does, but I have to open my Bible to hear Him!

> As the Father has loved me, so have I loved you...
> John 15:9

> Greater love hath no man than this, that a man lay down his life for his friends...
> John 15:13

> ...the Father himself loveth you, because ye have loved me...
> John 16:27

Father, I will that they also, whom thou hast given me, be with me where I am; that they may behold my glory, which thou hast given me...that the love wherewith thou has loved me may be in them, and I in them.

John 17:24, 26

Hymn:

"What wondrous love is this, O my soul, O my soul!
What wondrous love is this, O my soul!"

Fifty Eight

> The steps of a good man are ordered by the Lord: and he delighteth in his way. Though he fall, he shall not be utterly cast down: for the Lord upholdeth him with his hand.
>
> Psalm 37:23, 24

We are the "good man." We are "good" because God has made us good in His own eyes through the blood of Jesus.

The steps of a good man are ordered by the Lord... Our steps are ordered by the Lord.

...and he delighteth in his way. God is delighted with us. Think of that. God delights in you! Not only that, He delights in the way He has chosen for you. He knows it is a good way.

Though he fall, he shall not be utterly cast down... We'll never hit the bottom!...*for the Lord upholdeth him with his hand.* So take heart, my friend, for the God who delights in you will never let you hit the bottom!

Fifty Nine

> Many, O Lord my God, are thy wonderful works which thou hast done, and thy thoughts which are toward us: they cannot be reckoned up in order unto thee: if I would declare and speak of them, they are more than can be numbered.
>
> Psalm 40:5

God thinks about us a lot. But do we think about Him very much?

How precious to be on God's mind so often. Does it make you smile to think about that? It makes me smile and be so grateful that I serve a God who loves me that much. Think about all of God's creation and all of the people praying to Him every day, and yet, His thoughts about us...*are more than can be numbered.*

What an awesome and humbling thought! (And a lot to live up to!)

SIXTY

> By this I know that thou favorest me, because mine enemy doth not triumph over me.
>
> Psalm 41:11

When we think of "enemies," we usually think of wartime. Our enemy, however, could be whatever bothers us or interrupts our peace. Our health, someone in our family, our in-laws, or our finances, could be our enemy. Whatever we spend time worrying about could be our enemy, as well as how we feel about ourselves.

The scripture says that God can triumph over whatever is our enemy—if we will only let Him. God is a warrior for us. He can overcome every obstacle. In fact, He has already triumphed over our enemy through the blood of Jesus. Accept the battle victory that God has promised and has won. We can know that God favors us, because He will not let our enemy triumph over us!

Sixty One

I have a plant on the patio next to a kitchen window. One day as I was eating breakfast, I noticed a spider web woven between the plant and the kitchen window. I went outdoors, cleaned up the web, and watered the plant.

Several days later as I looked out of the window, the spider web was back. I said to myself, "It didn't do any good to clean up the web without getting rid of the *cause* of the web." My next step was to eliminate the spider that wove the web.

Our lives are like that. We try very hard to refrain from sinning, but until we deal with the cause of our sin, we will continue to displease God.

We need to search out the cause, lay it before the Lord to be forgiven and cleansed. Only then will we be free of the "spider webs" in our lives.

Sixty Two

My roses have had a particularly difficult time surviving this year. It seems that no matter how much care I give them, insects eat their leaves, and black spot spreads from plant to plant. Watering and spraying them has had little effect in fighting the enemy—still they grow and produce roses. Because of their scarcity, each rose is especially precious.

Does your life often seem like that? No matter how hard you try, and no matter how hard you pray, problems seem to bombard you on every side—and yet you grow, and you produce beautiful "roses" for others to see.

How our Heavenly Father must smile at us when He sees us carrying on, trusting Him, and loving Him even when He seems far away. However, He is not far away. He is very near and He watches over His children. And each beautiful "rose" produced in you is very special and beautiful to Him.

Song:

> "More than a song sung to praise him,
> More than just words I learn to say,
> If I'm to be an instrument worth using,
> Breathe life in me. Breathe life in me, I pray."

Sixty Three

As I was preparing for a walk one morning, I looked outside and noticed that there was a very strong wind—but the little hummingbirds were still chasing each other away from the bird feeders on the porch. I wondered how such a small bird could continue to fly in such a wind. Then I remembered that the birds would be migrating by the end of September, and their little wings would have to be very strong by then. Their "adversary," the wind, was actually helping to make them strong!

In our lives as well, God uses our tribulations to make us strong—strong in withstanding future stresses—strong in trusting and relying on Him—strong in understanding and being able to minister to others with similar needs.

Sometimes we think, "Lord, could I have a little *timeout* from so many problems?" but Paul says,

...I take pleasure in infirmities, in reproaches, in necessities, in persecutions, in distresses for Christ's sake; for when I am weak, then am I strong.
II Corinthians 12:10

So instead of complaining or feeling sorry for ourselves, we should take heart and say, "Lord, thank you for making me strong!"

SIXTY FOUR

Sometimes we use the expression, "Well, bless his heart!" The phrase is usually used when someone has worked very hard at something. They made a good effort but may not have quite gotten the job done.

God created us to bless His own heart. Yes, we can bless the heart of God.

> It blesses God's heart when we give sacrificially.
> It blesses God's heart when we praise Him unconditionally.
> It blesses God's heart when we cry over other people's misfortunes.
> It blesses God's heart when we love a child.
> It blesses God's heart when we sing to Him.
> It blesses God's heart when we come gratefully to Him in prayer.

Let's live this week seeking to "bless God's heart."

Bless the Lord, O my soul, and all that is within me, bless his holy name...

Psalm 103:1

...Inasmuch as ye have done it unto one of the least of these my brethren, ye have done it unto me.

Matthew 25:40

Sixty Five

This morning I was admiring some roses that I had picked yesterday. There were six of them from the same bush. They are Chicago Peace roses, and each one is different from the others. How interesting and unique they are.

Later, I called the pharmacy and a friend of mine answered. I recognized his voice and said, "Good morning. This is Patsy. I want to have a prescription refilled." When I hung up the phone, I thought, "I never did say my last name." He knew who I was. He recognized my voice too.

Not only do we all look different one from the other, but our fingerprints and our voices are unique. If my daughter or a good friend calls, I know who it is. I recognize her voice.

In the morning before I even get out of bed, I say, "Good morning, Lord." It doesn't occur to me that I need to add, "This is Patsy Cellier."

Isn't it a wonderful and awesome thought that God knows us *personally,* not as a "group of His children." We don't have to tell Him our name. He knew us before we were born. He made us and loves us. He has a plan for our lives. He watches over us and cares for us. He is a personal God for us.

> O Lord, thou hast searched me and known me...for there is not a word in my tongue, but lo, O Lord, thou knowest it altogether...whither shall I go from thy spirit...my substance was not hid from thee, when I was made in secret...how precious also are your thoughts unto me..."
>
> Psalm 139 (selected verses)

Sixty Six

What would you say if someone were to tell you that as a child of God, you receive preferential treatment? Would you point out all of the problems you're having and say, "Yow, right!" But have you also had a time in your life when you thought *your* problems were bad, until you came across someone who had a lot more problems than you did? What was your response? Mine was, "Wow! That makes my problems seem like nothing compared to theirs."

Do you give preferential treatment to anyone? Of course you do. If your child or grandchild needs (or wants) something, would you want to do it? Of course you would.

Matthew 7:11 says,

> If you then, being evil, know how to give good gifts unto your children, how much more shall your Father which is in heaven give good things to them that ask him?

Child of the King, see yourself as blessed each day. God *has* answered many of your prayers and is in the process of answering even more. Don't see yourself as a pauper or a slave. You're the King's kid. You eat up front at the King's banquet table!

Sixty Seven

One day as I was eating breakfast, a little wren flew onto the patio. He sometimes comes to check out a large airplane plant on the patio table. He hopped around the plant surveying it, then hopped inside the pot. I lost sight of him for a moment as he searched inside for any bugs that might be there. Suddenly, out he came and flew to the other side of the porch. I continued eating breakfast, then I heard a beautiful sound. I searched the patio with my eyes to find the little wren. There he was, perched on the top of a chair, head held high, little throat vibrating, singing a beautiful song.

I thought to myself, "Birds have a song to sing and so do people. How precious it is that we have that in common." One difference, however, is that people have a unique song to sing. Our song is to Jesus. Our song *is* Jesus.

The Singing ChurchWomen sing a song with the following words:

> "Jesus is the song of life,
> Jesus is the song of joy,
> Jesus is the song of love,
> Jesus gives His song *to me!*"

I hope Jesus is the song in your heart this week and that you'll be singing it all day long!

SIXTY EIGHT

During the fall season, we have the opportunity to reflect on the beauty of God's creation and to see an analogy of life.

Did you know that the beautiful red, yellow, brown, and plum colors of autumn have been in the leaf throughout the growing season of spring and summer? The colors have been hidden in the leaves by the chlorophyll working with the sunlight to give the tree its life. As the length of sunlight during the day diminishes, less and less chlorophyll is produced, and the beautiful hidden colors begin to be seen. Isn't that amazing? It is to me.

Next, the leaves die and fall off the tree. The tree appears to be dead, but life is still inside. The dead leaves lie on the ground, and I feel sad because this season has passed. Then I realize that those dead leaves will have an influence on the future life of the tree. As the leaves decay, they become a part of the soil that will give life to the tree as it begins a new growing season!

Dear friends, the influence of your life will live on, way past your living on the earth. Your prayers, encouragement, good deeds, and money used for God's kingdom will outlive you. Your advice and love will live on in the memories of those who have known you.

What an awesome God we serve. He has a plan for the seasons and a plan for our lives. We are both beautiful in His sight!

> He hath made everything beautiful in his time...
> Ecclesiastes 3:11

Sixty Nine

This morning as I was reading one of my favorite verses in Proverbs, *Trust in the Lord with all your heart...* I paused to think about the word "trust," wondering what God really meant by that word. I remembered a situation that happened when I was a little girl.

When I was young, my daddy built a playhouse for me in our backyard. I loved making mud pies and playing with my neighbor, Sissy. One day, for some reason, I climbed onto the roof of the playhouse and was afraid to climb down. I called for help and my daddy came running. I remember looking down at my "little daddy," five feet six inches, weighing about 135 pounds. Daddy told me to jump down, and he would catch me. I wondered how he could possibly catch me without dropping me. He urged me until I finally jumped into his arms. He caught me and didn't even fall down.

That's what God wants us to do—to jump into His arms. He will catch us, and He'll never fall down! That's trusting Him with all of our hearts.

Seventy

> ...He delivered me, because he delighted in me.
>
> Psalm 18:19b

Have you ever thought about the times God has delivered you? Have you ever been in your car when someone cut right in front of you, and you wondered how he kept from hitting you? Have you been in a room with a group of sick people or had someone sneeze directly in your face? You probably thought, "Well, I got that one!" but you didn't. Have you prayed for "impossible" things only to see them happen?

Sometimes I pause and just thank God for all the times He has delivered me, and I didn't even know it. There may be thousands of times.

Take a moment to thank God for delivering you. He may even show you some of the things you missed!

> For who is God save the Lord? Or who is a rock save our God? He maketh my feet like hinds feet, and setteth me upon my high places. Thou hast enlarged my steps under me, that my feet did not slip.
>
> Psalm 18:31, 33, 36

Seventy One

Jesus is like the trash man. Did that get your attention? Follow this analogy: At our house the day before garbage pick-up, Clayton goes through the house gathering the trash. He starts with the big bag of trash in the kitchen. He stuffs the trash down as far as he can and proceeds to the bathrooms and bedrooms. After gathering all the trash, he takes it to the trash container.

Now, picture Jesus going to your house and to each house on your block. He proceeds to each house in your city, your state, your country, the whole world gathering trash. That's what Jesus did, and he carried it all by Himself. We call the trash "sin." Jesus took all of the sin with Him to the cross. With His death, "Poof!" all of it was gone—but not quite all—only the sin of those who accept Him as Savior. *Our* "trash" is gone (forgiven), but some remains.

Those who reject Jesus still carry around their own trash. What a heavy load. Who do you know that is carrying around all their trash? Talk to them about Jesus.

> But he was wounded and bruised for our sins. He was chastised that we might have peace; He was lashed... and we are healed! We are the ones who strayed away like sheep! We, who left God's paths to follow our own. Yet God laid on him the guilt and sins of every one of us!
>
> Isaiah 53:5, 6 (TLB)

Seventy Two

During the summer months, we enjoyed the hummingbirds that fed from the feeders on our patio. By the first of October, they were gone. We hated to see them go.

In the summer, most of the prettier birds like the cardinals and blue jays were off raising families and eating insects and seeds in the woods. But we always had the sparrows. Clayton thought they must surely be breeding at our house. We would see thirty or more at a time in the evening. They were almost a nuisance.

After the hummingbirds left, many sparrows were gone as well. We were down to only a few. I began to miss even the sparrows, because I like to see birds at the feeder.

I thought about the little things in life that God does for us, which we take so much for granted. Jesus talked about the sparrows. They were even important to Him.

As I began to appreciate the sparrows, I was privileged to have a little tufted titmouse visit me. He landed on a patio chair with his blue-gray feathers, a touch of orange on his tummy, and a colic of feathers sticking up on his head. Later, a female cardinal came to drink at the birdbath near the porch.

Maybe God wants us to recognize and be thankful for the day to day gifts He sends before He'll send the more obvious ones.

Let's be thankful for the "sparrows" of life. They're all around us. And they're really very beautiful.

Seventy Three

As I was reading Isaiah 55:1, this is what the KJV said:

> Ho, every one that thirsteth, come ye to the waters, and he that hath no money; come ye, buy, and eat; yea, come buy wine and milk without money and without price.

This is what the verse meant to me: "Look here, all of you who are thirsty; you who have lost all hope; you feel that you are dying in your spirit. Come to Me. I not only have water for you, but a flowing fountain. Come and drink all you need.

If you have no money, no way to keep your very life, that's okay. Come as if you had all the money in the world. Not only will you find all that you need in Me, but it will be like wine and milk: wine for the returning of your joy, and milk for good health.

Come, for all that I offer is fulfilling, and it is free anyway."

Do we need this message at Christmas with all the hustle and bustle and stress to get everything done and make everyone happy? I do.

It brings peace to my heart to know that everything I need, I can find in Him.

So come. Come to the manger. See the newborn king with all the possibilities we will later realize.

Come. See His glory—and be at peace.

SEVENTY FOUR

Mary didn't expect to be told that she would be the mother of the Son of God.

Elizabeth and Zacharias didn't expect to be the parents of the forerunner of the Messiah.

The shepherds didn't expect to be visited by a host of angels in the middle of the night.

The Wise Men didn't expect to see an unusual star in the sky which would lead them to the Promised One.

I didn't expect to be at my grandson's junior high basketball game and overhear a conversation in the bathroom. We were visitors in a public school. I went to the bathroom and heard a number of girls talking. Several girls were trying to calm and console one of their friends who was crying angrily. The girl talked about how people were treating her that night. She also talked about her dad mistreating her. This went on for several minutes. She was very angry and upset. I listened and waited in the stall. When it was quiet, I stepped out.

There stood a beautiful, red-faced, tearful young lady in a cheerleader uniform. I asked God what I should do. The girl and I looked at each other, and I said, "I can offer you a hug." I took a step forward, and she came toward me and let me hold her.

I talked quietly to her, and told her that it was sometimes tough growing up, but God loved her. I looked at her and encouraged her to talk to a trusted adult if she needed to. Then I held her again and prayed for her. When I finished, she seemed calm and peaceful. We smiled at each other, and I left the room.

Expect God to use you and He will,
even when you least expect it.

Seventy Five

Jesus' life on earth began with a miracle. He was born of a virgin with God Himself as His father.

The events of that first Christmas are so compelling as we rehearse them in our minds. Jesus was born in Bethlehem to fulfill prophesy. The shepherds were visited by the angels. The Wise Men in another country saw the star and made their way to Jesus.

Had it not been for the cross, however, all of this might have been forgotten in the annals of history. Who Jesus was, what He taught, what He did, how and why He died, were all determined by His heavenly Father when He sent Him to the earth. What a victory the Father must have felt when He called Jesus home at the Resurrection. He must have greeted Him saying, "Well done, My Son!"

None of us will have accomplished what Jesus did, but the Father will gladly call us home one day too. I hope He says to us, "Well done!"

Song:

> "Jesus paid it all,
> All to Him I owe.
> Sin had left a crimson stain.
> He washed it white as snow."

Seventy Six

At this time of the year, it's time to bring the house plants back indoors before they freeze. A large spider plant sitting on the patio table has been making "babies" throughout the summer. Now comes the time to prune the plant and select a few of the very best "babies" to put together to make a new potted plant. I always hate to discard any living thing, but I am limited in space for a new plant. I have to select a few and discarded the rest of them.

I'm so glad God doesn't deal with us that way. He says "whosoever" may come. All are included. The only requirement is accepting Jesus as Savior and Lord.

I'm glad I don't have to measure up through my own righteousness or goodness. Jesus covers it all.

> For God so loved the world, that he gave his only begotten Son, that whosoever believeth in him should not perish, but have everlasting life.
>
> John 3:16

Seventy Seven

I am a person who likes to know that things will work out in the future even before I get there. The future might be tomorrow, or next week, or later. Because there's no assurance regarding the future, I end up worrying about something.

Jesus' teaching is clear about this in Matthew's account of the Sermon on the Mount.

God wants us to trust Him to provide not only for today, but for our tomorrows. This is difficult for me. But for the "moments" that I do this, I am at peace. I wish my "moments" would stretch into days, and days into weeks, and so on.

We must set our minds on Christ and remember the lilies and the sparrows. God will provide for us, even more than He does for them.

HE LOVES US THAT MUCH.

SEVENTY EIGHT

Psalm 121 reads as follows:

> I will lift up mine eyes unto the hills from whence cometh my help. My help cometh from the Lord, which made heaven and earth. He will not suffer thy foot to be moved: He that keepeth thee will not slumber... The Lord is thy keeper: the Lord is thy shade upon thy right hand. The sun shall not smite thee by day, nor the moon by night. The Lord shall preserve thee from all evil: he shall preserve thy soul. The Lord shall preserve thy going out and thy coming in from this time forth, and even forevermore.

Is God there for you? Is God *going* to be there for you?

THE ANSWER IS A DEFINITE YES!

Seventy Nine

Have you ever bagged up items to give away or prepared to sell things at a garage sale, only to go back, rummage through them, and end up keeping them?

Don't do that with your worries and fears. Bag them all up. Tie them tightly at the top. Throw them over your shoulder and carry them to Jesus. Lay them down at His feet. Walk away and don't go back. You'll never need them again. They are gone.

What a relief you'll feel. How light your steps will be—how broad your smile!

Song:

> "Give them all,
> Give them all,
> Give them all to Jesus.
> And He will turn your sorrows into joy."

Eighty

I prefer sunny days over cloudy days. I can tell the passing of time better, and it just gives me a lift when it's sunny outside.

This morning as I was sitting on the bed putting on my tennis shoes, the sun was shining directly through the window onto my face. I smiled, thinking of how the sun blesses me.

God placed the earth in the universe in just the right position, so that we would not be "burned up" by being too close to the sun, nor too far away so that we would "freeze." The sun not only gives light and warmth, but growing things can't live without it. It indeed gives *physical* life to all mankind.

Now consider this: mankind cannot have *spiritual* life without the "Son" of God!

It's interesting to me that in God's creation, He named the "bright light" in the sky, the "sun," and when He sent the real "Light of the World," He called Him "His Son."

Eighty One

● ● ● ● ● ● ● ● ● ●

Have you ever noticed when driving on some highways that the trees are all bent in a certain direction?

Trees are bent by strong winds over a long period of time, but roots growing deep into the ground anchor the trees and keep them from falling over.

If we are to withstand the "strong winds" of time, we must have strong roots. The Bible is our root system. If we are rooted and grounded in the Word of God, we can withstand even the strongest winds of time.

> ...be strengthened with might by his Spirit in the inner man...that ye might be filled with all the fullness of God...rooted and grounded in love...
>
> Ephesians 3:16–19

EIGHTY TWO

When someone hurts our feelings or treats us unfairly, we have a choice to make. We can be angry or resentful. We can withdraw or flee, or we can forgive. Only one of these pleases God. Only one of these opens the door for reconciliation. Only one of these brings peace—forgiveness.

Do it quickly. You'll save yourself a whole lot of grief!

> Let all bitterness, and wrath, and anger, and clamour, and evil speaking, be put away from you, with all malice. And be ye kind one to another; tenderhearted, forgiving one another, even as God for Christ's sake hath forgiven you.
>
> Ephesians 4:31, 32

Eighty Three

When things seem out of control—they are not! If you're looking to yourself to solve the problem, good luck. If you expect other people to fix it, "not gonna happen." If you're looking for help from God, you're looking in the right place!

> When the enemy shall come in like a flood, the Spirit of the Lord shall lift up a standard against him.
>
> Isaiah 59:19b

> Fear not, for I have redeemed you; I have called you by name, you are mine. When you pass through the waters I will be with you; and through the rivers, they shall not overwhelm you. When you walk through the fire, you shall not be burned, and the flame shall not consume you...Because you are precious in my eyes, and honored and I love you.
>
> Isaiah 43:1b, 2, 4b

Eighty Four

> A soft answer turneth away wrath...
> Proverbs 15:1a

Have you ever tried using this principle to see if it works?

I had an opportunity to use this scriptural advice this week when I called to renew an EMSA membership for my mom. The EMSA representative who answered the telephone seemed irritated at my questions. She began talking faster and louder to me. I caught myself doing the same. I immediately slowed my speech and lowered my tone, adding apologies and appreciation as I proceeded. By the end of our conversation, she was talking cordially to me as well.

I find that scriptural advice is actually a command that God expects us to follow. It is also good for our own health. His Word says the following:

My son, attend to my words; incline thine ear unto my sayings. Let them not depart from thine eyes; keep them in the midst of thine heart. For they are life unto those that find them, and health to all their flesh.
Proverbs 4:20–22

The next time you find yourself in a confrontational situation, follow God's Word and watch the results!

Eighty Five

> ...giving thanks always for all things unto God and the Father in the name of our Lord Jesus Christ.
>
> Ephesians 5:20

I was looking forward to Spring Break so that I could slow down a little and not be on a tight schedule. I wanted to have time to get back to some exercise walking that I had neglected—so what happened? I got up Monday morning, and my right knee felt like I had pulled something. On went the old elastic knee brace that I hadn't needed for a long time. I nursed my ailment all day, trying not to complain. When I went to bed that night, I realized that instead of grumbling, I should have been thanking God for the things that are *right* in my life.

The following were my thoughts: "O Lord, I'm so sorry that I don't spend enough time thanking You for all the things that are *right* in my life. If I started right now and continued every moment for the rest of my life, I wouldn't have enough time to thank You for all the blessings during my lifetime..." I fell asleep before I could finish thanking Him.

Maybe you have some things for which you need to thank God. As you begin, you'll find more than you realized!

> Whoso offereth praise glorifieth me...
> Psalm 50:23

Eighty Six

> He that hath pity upon the poor lendeth unto the Lord; and that which he hath given will he pay him again.
>
> Proverbs 19:17

As I read this proverb, I was reminded of a time when I was a young wife and mother. We lived on Clayton's teacher salary of $3,500 a year.

I had a burden to give $50 to a particular cause. That was a lot of money at that time, but I wanted to be obedient to the Lord, so I gave it.

Some time later a friend of mine called. She was having a Christmas party at her house, and she asked if I would come and sing for her guests. I did so.

When I left her house that night, she handed me an envelope—there was my $50! I knew it was from the Lord, showing me that I never could out-give Him.

WHEN WE GIVE TO OTHERS, WE TRULY GIVE TO HIM.

Eighty Seven

Picture with me the following scene: Loving arms take Jesus down from the cross and gently carry Him to the tomb. Having washed and wrapped the body, the men stand looking down at the lifeless form, tears filling their eyes. They stand in disbelief, stunned and deeply saddened. Reluctantly, they leave. A huge stone is rolled in place covering the entrance to the tomb.

The remainder of that day passes, then the next—but on the morning of the third day inside the tomb, the shrouded figure moves. His eyes open. He sits up. He stands. The linens fall off—and *Jesus walks out.*

He didn't need the stone to be moved, because He could have walked through it. It was moved so that others could see in! And that's what happened. Women arrived to find the tomb empty. *Jesus was alive*—and with that, the *world* was alive, and *we* are alive!

The job was done. The ransom was paid. The victory was won, and we are the recipients. With *His* resurrection, *we* have *Eternal Life!*

THANK YOU, JESUS!

Eighty Eight

Last week I was at Tinker Elementary where I taught until I retired. One of our long term teachers had just been sent home from the hospital, basically to die. Doctors could not do anything for her. Three teachers had made a quilt to give her, and everyone was invited to sign it. I signed it, "Love you, Patsy Cellier."

After school, there was a sign up sheet for anyone willing to take a turn sitting with the teacher to give the family a break. I thought, "There's no way I can work that into my already busy schedule," so, I didn't sign.

That night as I was reading and praying for the teacher, I realized that I must not really love her, because love is shown by action—

> God so loved the world that He gave…What? His only begotten Son…
>
> John 3:16

I'm going to *find* the time to sit with my friend, because *love* behaves that way.

IF WE REALLY LOVE GOD, WE'LL *FIND* TIME FOR HIM TOO!

EIGHTY NINE

Honoring our father and mother is not an option. It's a commandment. Jesus didn't do away with the Ten Commandments; He simplified and extended them. He simplified them when He said,

> Thou shalt love the Lord thy God with all thy heart, and with all thy soul, and with all thy mind...Thou shalt love thy neighbor as thyself. Matthew 22:38, 39
> He extended them when He said, Ye have heard that it was said...But I say unto you...
>
> Matthew 5:27, 28

For some people it is easy to honor their parents. They deserve it. But for others it is more difficult.

God's Word remains the same. When we honor our parents, we are honoring God and obeying Him.

Those who have lost their parents may need to honor them by forgiving them (or themselves).

Ninety

We don't like problems, but problems build character.

> Dear brothers, is your life full of difficulties and temptations? Then be happy, for when the way is rough, your patience has a chance to grow. So let it grow, and don't try to squirm out of your problems. For when your patience is finally in full bloom, then you will be ready for anything, strong in character, full and complete.
>
> James 1:2–4 (TLB)

Whatever major problem you are facing, the one you most wish would go away, be thankful for it, because God is maturing your faith through it. You are privileged to experience a small portion of what Christ went through.

Ninety One

A week ago, my son-in-law had arthroscopic knee surgery. It was quite extensive. The first week Greg was recovering very well, but then he noticed that the leg was red and was hurting again. The doctor wanted to see him. There was some concern that there might be infection in the bone. We began to pray.

> The Lord put the following scripture on my heart: I have seen his ways, and will heal him: I will lead him also, and restore comforts unto him and to his mourners. I create the fruit of the lips; Peace, peace to him that is far off, and to him that is near, saith the Lord; and I will heal him.
>
> Isaiah 57:18, 19

I realized that God has the final word. He had the "beginning" Word. He will have the *last* "final" Word, and He has the final word in each of our circumstances.

The doctor said Greg was recovering nicely, and he didn't see a problem.

Thank you, Lord!

Ninety Two

Sometimes we get frustrated when we can't contact someone on the telephone. We call and get the answering machine. We call again, and still there is no one at home—but God is always available when we want to talk to Him. He knows we're "going to call," and He knows what we want to talk to Him about as well. He is always "home."

> Call unto me and I will answer thee, and show thee great and mighty things, which thou knowest not.
>
> Jeremiah 33:3

> And it shall come to pass, that before they call, I will answer: and while they are yet speaking, I will hear.
>
> Isaiah 65:21

> He shall call upon me, and I will answer him; I will be with him in trouble: I will deliver him, and honor him.
>
> Psalm 91:15

Ninety Three

Sometimes we have to go through dark times in our lives to see the real light coming through.

The other night I stepped out onto the back porch and looked up into the sky. Sunset was nearly completed, and the sky was darkening. The crescent moon was brilliantly lit up, and two stars shone brightly. Ever so often I caught a glimpse of another star in the sky, but when I looked, it was gone. I decided to come back outside later when the darkness had fully fallen.

Before I went to bed that night, I stepped out onto the porch again and looked skyward. The night was brilliantly aglow with light in the blackened sky, and I thought, "The darker the night, the clearer the light."

Difficult times in our lives are not fun, but sometimes the only way to see the light clearly is in the midst of darkness.

> ...I am the light of the world; he that followeth me shall not walk in darkness, but shall have the light of life.
>
> John 8:12

NINETY FOUR

What's in a name? Answer: An identity.

After my marriage, it was important to my mom that I retain my maiden name as part of my signature. However, I didn't see the appropriateness of doing so. Therefore, I might be known as Patsy Cellier, Patricia A. Cellier, Patricia S. (Shaw) Cellier, or Patsy S. Cellier.

In 1996, however, my parents had a Living Trust drawn up with daddy and me as trustees so that I could take care of mom in the event of his passing. At that time, I became aware of the importance of including my maiden name on legal documents, so that my full identity would be evident.

As I recently thought about the name identity, I realized that as Christians, we find our most important, lasting, and final identity in the Lord Jesus. Each of us, therefore, might sign our names including a reference to Christ. I would become Patricia Shaw Cellier Christian! Notice that the final name is God's name, because that's my ultimate identity.

Fear not: for I have redeemed thee; I have called thee by name; thou art mine.

Isaiah 43:1b

And if children, then heirs; heirs of God, and joint-heirs with Christ...

Romans 8:17

...Behold the tabernacle of God is with men, and he will dwell with them, and they shall be his people, and God himself shall be with them, and be their God.

Revelation 21:3

Ninety Five

Recently our Sunday School lessons have been centered on the love languages of God and how we can use those languages in dealing with others. One of the languages is service.

As I thought about my own life, I realized that even small services can show love for Christ. The Lord brought the following examples to my mind:

One day as I was shopping at the grocery store, I turned up the aisle to find an older man standing there. He seemed to want to talk. I learned that it was his ninetieth birthday that day. I asked if he was going to have a party. He said, "No." Thinking that was a sad thing, I asked his name and began singing "Happy Birthday" to him. Congratulating him, I proceeded down the aisle. I turned back around, and he was still standing there smiling.

Another day, a sudden downpour began as I was leaving Wal-Mart. A middle-aged lady was standing outside looking perplexed. I offered to share my umbrella and walk her to her car. She cheerfully obliged.

Last week I was at the doctor's office. I followed a young lady on crutches and struck up a conversation with her. I held the door open and offered to drive her to her car. She declined, but appreciated the offer.

Sometimes a simple smile and greeting can even bless someone's day!

> So in everything, do to others what you would have them do to you.
>
> Matthew 7:12 (NIV)

Ninety Six

For ten days I was taking medication that was intended to help me, but instead, it was making me worse. My mind was filled with worries and anxious thoughts. I wanted my own mind back!

A friend reminded me that as a believer, I had the "mind of Christ." I began repeating that over and over to myself and claimed scripture for my healing. The doctor took me off the medication, and I am doing well, but the thought of the mind of Christ has remained with me. How would Jesus feel in the circumstances of our lives today?

When Jesus walked on earth with our earthly frailties, I can't believe that He was worried or fretful or had misgivings concerning the future. He knew that each day was in the Father's hand, and the Father would be there and provide. He knew both the awesome power of God and the limitlessness of His love—but we know this too.

So whatever challenges the day brings, we must say to ourselves and to the enemy, "I have the mind of Christ!" Satan must surely be stunned at that word of faith—I love it when he loses!

> For who hath known the mind of the Lord, that he may instruct him? But we have the mind of Christ.
> I Corinthians 2:16

> For God hath not given us the spirit of fear; but of power and of love, and of a sound mind.
> II Timothy 1:7

Ninety Seven

We need to develop a listening heart.

As I sat on my patio eating breakfast one morning, I noticed that it was especially noisy outside. A neighbor was mowing his lawn. An airplane flew over the house. The man next door was edging grass near the curb—then suddenly the noises stopped. I sat listening. Now I could hear a cardinal singing from the top of a nearby tree. Crows in the distance were calling to and answering one another. I heard the sound of hummingbird wings fluttering at the porch feeder. I sat quietly listening.

Sounds of nature have a calming effect on me, but listening to God's voice is not only calming, but encouraging, and gives me a sense of direction.

In our busy schedules, we need to take time to listen to the sounds of nature, but even more time listening to the voice of God.

Be still and know that I am God.

Psalm 46:10

I will hear what God the Lord will speak: for he will speak peace unto his people.

Psalm 85:8

NINETY EIGHT

Following his winning the eleventh British Open Golf Championship, Tiger Woods sought out runner up, Chris DeMarco, and his dad, Rich. Tiger had lost his dad in May, and Rich DeMarco had lost his wife suddenly in July.

Woods is quoted as telling the dad, "I know what you're going through. My dad was my best friend, and your wife was your best friend."

If you have a best friend, you are very fortunate. You may have many friends, but to have someone whom you can really trust is a precious gift.

The Bible tells us that *There is a friend that sticketh closer than a brother.* Proverbs 18:24 and *Jesus was called a friend of sinners.* Luke 17:34b

BE CLOSE FRIENDS WITH JESUS. WALK SHOULDER TO SHOULDER WITH YOUR SAVIOR!

Ninety Nine

As I was taking a walk one morning, I observed a Mockingbird sitting on the top of a telephone pole. Mockingbirds are very interesting birds. Not only do they copy or "mock" other birds' songs, but they have a very interesting flying somersault that they do, flying in the air, turning a somersault, and landing where they started. As I listened to the Mockingbird rehearse his repertoire of songs, and I watched him practice his somersaults that morning, I thought of how happy he seemed. He greeted the morning with a song and a leap into the air!

Do you get up in the morning singing, "This is the day that the Lord has made. I will be glad and rejoice in it"?

My doctor once told me that happiness is a "choice" we make. Our spouse can't make us happy. Our children can't make us happy. Happiness is a choice only *we* can make.

So are you going to get up in the morning and say, "I wonder what's going to happen to me today," or "This is the day the Lord has made. I will rejoice and be glad in it"? The choice is up to you!

> Rejoice in the Lord, always; again I say, rejoice!
> Philippians 4:4

One Hundred

Birds have a wonderful way of shedding water. Robins love to play in the lawn sprinkler, (then eat worms that surface afterwards). Birds get in the birdbath, stick their heads in the water, fluff it on their wings, and shake it off, and you never see a mother duck toweling down her offspring!

I wish words were as easy to shed. Words seem to stay in our minds even when we try to *shed* them. Sometimes words spoken in kindness or for encouragement remain to bless us. Other words, spoken in criticism or blame, continue to hurt.

We cannot control the words that others speak, but we can guard our own. It's a full-time job, but a necessary one!

> A soft answer turneth away wrath: but grievous words stir up anger.
>
> Proverbs 15:11

One Hundred One

Picture yourself wrapping a large birthday present for a friend. You've picked out your favorite wrapping paper. You've strung the wide satin ribbon around the box and topped it with a large bow. Standing back, you look at your gift. You can hardly wait to give it. Finally the time comes for you to present it to your friend—but your friend won't accept it. Think how you would feel—that's how God felt.

God gave to the world the very best gift anyone could ever give—salvation.

> For God so loved the world that he gave his only begotten son...
>
> John 3:16.

Now think of God's delight when *you* accepted His gift. He gave you His best gift and *you* received it. You blessed God's heart!

Epilogue

Dear Friend,

After reading this book, you may realize that *you* also want to bless the Father's heart by accepting Jesus as *your* Savior. If that is true, you may want to say a simple prayer such as the following:

"Dear Lord, I recognize that I am a sinner, and I indeed need a Savior. I realize that only through the sacrificial blood of Jesus can my salvation be possible. I repent of my sins and give my life to You. Come dwell in me and make me a new creature in Christ Jesus. Thank You, Lord. I now belong to You."

For all have sinned, and come short of the glory of God; Being justified freely by his grace through the redemption that is in Christ Jesus...

Romans 3:23

For by grace ye are saved through faith; and that not of yourselves: it is a gift of God: lest any man should boast.

Ephesians 2:8, 9

For whosoever shall call upon the name of the Lord shall be saved.

Romans 10:13

There is therefore now no condemnation to them which are in Christ Jesus, who walk not after the flesh, but after the Spirit.

Romans 8:1

Therefore, if any man be in Christ, he is a new creature: old things are passed away; behold, all things are become new.

II Corinthians 5:17

Now, Friend, ask God to guide you to a church fellowship where the Bible is taught as the only truth and Jesus as the only Savior.